**99 Questions for Global Friends**
Quality Conversation Starters for Friends
From Different Places

Self Published
Qingdao, China
*www.thecultureblend.com*

"You can tell whether a man is clever by his answers.  You can tell whether a man is wise by his questions"

*Naguib Mahfouz*

# INTRODUCTION

**Thanks for taking a look at this incredibly simple little book.**

If you have cross-cultural friends then this was written especially for you.

# This book was written for rich people.

Billionaires with private jets are welcome but this is designed for people far wealthier than that.

**The target audience here is people blessed with the treasure of knowing other people who are different from them. People from a different place with a different story and a different perspective.**

This book is about digging one level deeper into the cross-cultural relationships that you already have and seeing the world through a different set of eyes.

That's it.

The responses will be both right and wrong. Some will be based on cold hard facts and others will be total, opinionated conjecture.

None of that matters.

You might be shocked. It's likely that you'll laugh. It's possible that you'll cry but it is inevitable that you will come away more connected with a deeper grasp on something that you thought you already understood.

One quick warning before you begin.

**Don't look for answers.**

Answers (especially correct ones) lie to us. They leave us believing that there is nothing more to ask which is NEVER, EVER true.

These 99 questions are a starting point not a finish line. They offer a window into people who can open the door to new places where exploration can happen and understanding can begin.

*Each question is accompanied by eight others just to keep the conversation moving but don't stop there.*

*Write the rest of the book.*

# If you are rich enough to have friends who are not like you, pick a number between 1 and 99 or just flip through and pick your favorite . . . ask . . . listen . . . repeat.

*You can check out the other books in the*
**99 Questions** *series along with more great resources
and insights into cross-cultural life at*


# www.thecultureblend.com

## SOME GUIDELINES

- Value the conversation NOT the answer.

- Use the 8 accompanying question to discover more.

- Include your own questions. What are you curious to know?

- If a question doesn't apply, change it or move on. Don't stress about it.

- Listen intently. Share vulnerably. Repeat consistently.

## Adjust each question until it fits you perfectly.

# 1

# What does red mean? What about blue? Yellow? Green?

What emotions do colors make you feel?

What events do colors represent?

What places do you think of?

What colors are good or bad?

What people do you think of?

What does black represent?

Who does white represent?

How has this changed over time?

# 2

# What is the preparation for a big meal like at your home?

Who does the cooking?

How long does it take?

How many people are in the kitchen?

What do you talk about?

What do the non-cooking people do?

What dishes are prepared?

Who cleans up after?

What do you drink while you prepare food?

# 3

# What do older people from your country think about people from my country?

What stereotypes might they have?

Where might their ideas come from?

How do they differ from younger generations?

Are younger people embarrassed by older?

Where do older people get together?

When is a person considered old?

Do you agree or disagree?

How has this changed over time?

# 4

# What do children want to be when they grow up?

What are the most desirable jobs?

What makes them desirable?

Is it different for boys and girls?

Do children want to be famous?

Do children want to be rich?

Are children encouraged to pursue their dreams?

What are the least desirable jobs?

How has this changed over time?

# 5

# What is an average day like for a 10 year old?

What is education like?

How do they learn?

What do they play?

What is fun?

What is difficult?

What are they not allowed to do?

What would they eat every day if they could?

How has this changed over time?

# 6

# How do people get married?

Is there a ceremony?

Who is invited?

How do people celebrate?

Who pays?

What do people eat?

How long does it last?

What colors are important?

Is it religious?

# 7

# What happens to a person's body when they die?

Is there a funeral or ceremony?

How do people mourn?

Are they buried?

Are they cremated?

What happens to their possessions?

Are there laws about burying etc.?

Are there colors that are associated with death?

Is it different for different people?

# 8

# Who is a hero?

Who do people respect?

What did this person do?

What are some stories about this person?

What makes them a hero?

Are there stories that have been exaggerated?

Does everyone agree that they are a hero?

When did they live?

What was life like for them?

# 9

# What is rude?

What would a mother tell her child is rude?

What do people think when they see rudeness?

How do people react?

Do you tell someone they are rude?

What kind of people are rude?

What noises are rude?

What is rude to say?

How do you learn what is rude?

# 10

# How do you know if someone is rich?

What is a rich person's appearance?

Do they speak differently?

What kind of clothing does a rich person wear?

What kind of transportation do they use?

Are they seen favorably or unfavorably?

What attitudes do rich people have?

Are rich people friendly?

How has this changed over time?

# 11

# How do you know if someone is dangerous?

What does a dangerous person look like?

Why are they dangerous?

Are they old or young?

What are you afraid they will do?

How do you respond when you see them?

What should you not do?

Who protects you from dangerous people?

How has this changed over time?

# 12

# What are the most important days of the year?

What do you celebrate?

Are there important days for your country?

How do you celebrate those days?

What do you eat when you celebrate?

What stories are there about special days?

What colors are associated with special days?

What songs are associated with special days?

Which days do families get together?

# 13

## How would your life be different if you were the same age 50 years ago?

What would your home be like?

What would your family be like?

How would your clothing be different?

How would your hair be different?

What kind of food would you eat?

What was different about your government?

What would have been better about your life?

What would have been worse?

# 14

# How old are people when they get married?

How are marriages decided?

What do people think if someone never marries?

Is there pressure to get married?

Where does pressure come from?

What age is too young to get married?

What are the laws about getting married?

What is the perfect age to get married?

How has this changed over time?

# 15

# What happens when a woman finds out she is pregnant?

What emotions does she feel?

Who does she tell first?

Who does she tell next?

How will people respond ?

How is the birth celebrated?

Who is the happiest?

What kind of support does a pregnant mother get?

Are there laws about pregnancy?

# 16

## What does a woman do to make herself beautiful?

Who does she want to be beautiful for?

What occasions would she want to be beautiful?

What are some different opinions about beauty?

What is not beautiful?

What services are available for beauty?

What products are available for beauty?

Does this change after she is married?

How has this changed over time?

# 17

# What does a man do to make himself attractive?

Who does he want to be attractive to?

Which men are most concerned about looking good?

What are opinions about what makes men attractive?

What is not attractive?

What services might a man use to be attractive?

What products might a man use to be attractive?

Does this change after he is married?

How has this changed over time?

# 18

# What games do children play?

What are games that most children would know?

Are there different versions?

What age do you learn these games?

Are they specific to boys or girls?

When do you play these games?

Do children play dangerous games?

Do children play team games?

Are games competitive or simply fun?

# 19

# What are the differences between your generation and your parent's generation?

What opinions are different?

How is the economy different?

How are politics different?

How is education different?

What does their generation think of yours?

What does your generation think of theirs?

What do they not understand about you?

What do you not understand about them?

# 20

# Which three sports to people in your country enjoy the most?

Which is the most important? Second?

Who plays them?

Do you have professional teams?

When do you learn how to play?

What are the rules?

Are there traditions associated with the sports?

How do people celebrate a win?

How do people react to a loss?

# 21

# What is polite?

What actions are polite?

How do you learn what politeness is?

How is politeness rewarded?

What is impolite?

What words are polite?

Is this different in different parts of your country?

How has politeness changed over time?

Who is known for being polite?

# 22

# What is something that people should not eat?

What is illegal to eat?

What is socially unacceptable to eat?

What do some people like but most don't?

Do people eat differently in different regions?

What is culturally unacceptable to eat?

What is disgusting?

What is too expensive to eat?

What has changed over time?

# 23

# What is a great job?

What are jobs that many people want?

What makes it so great?

Is money or happiness more important?

What job requires the most education?

What job requires the least education?

What is the schedule of a great job?

What is a great salary?

What other benefits come with a great job?

# 24

# What is a bad job?

What jobs do no one want?

What makes it so bad?

Can you get out of a bad job?

How do you find a better job?

What is a bad work schedule?

Are there embarrassing jobs?

What is a bad salary?

Who does the worst jobs?

# 25

# What is difficult for a 16 year old?

Does a 16 year old have pressure?

Where does pressure come from?

What social problems do they have?

What school problems?

What do they think about?

What do they do in their free time?

What emotions do they have?

What do they get angry about?

# 26

# How do you train a child to use the toilet?

What methods do you use?

Who does the training?

When does training start?

How long does it take?

Are there products that help?

What happens when a child has a hard time?

How old is too old to not be trained?

Are there different methods used in your country?

# 27

# Who are great artists from your country?

What types of art are famous in your country?

What role does art play in your history?

Do you have museums?

Are there controversial artists?

How are artists perceived?

What does traditional music sound like?

What is traditional dance?

How has the art of your country changed over time?

# 28

# How do you communicate with your hands?

What are some common hand gestures?

How do you communicate approval?

How do you communicate anger?

Are some hand gestures bad?

How would you point at something?

What gestures are considered rude?

How do you count with your hands?

Is it common to use your hands while speaking?

# 29

# What noises do animals make?

Dog?

Cat?

Cow?

Chicken?

Elephant?

Sheep/Goat?

Horse?

Others?

# 30

# What do people do when they get old?

What do people do when they stop working?

Where do they live?

When do people stop working?

How do they support themselves?

What do they do for fun?

What happens when they live alone?

Who takes care of them?

What is the biggest challenge?

# 31

# Who takes care of children?

Who watches children during the day?

What role does extended family play?

Who watches children when parents go out?

When do children start school?

Are there services that watch children?

Is child care expensive?

Is it common to have a hired helper?

When is a child old enough to stay home alone?

# 32

# What is a good wedding gift?

Do you give gifts for a wedding?

Is money a good gift?

How expensive should a gift be?

Do you take a gift to a wedding or send it?

What is a bad wedding gift?

Is it ok to ask for specific gifts?

Who receives the gift?

How do you present the gift?

# 33

## What is lucky?

What items etc. are considered to be lucky?

Do you know why they are considered lucky?

Are any numbers considered lucky?

What is considered bad luck?

Are certain days considered lucky?

How much do people believe in luck?

Are lucky things more expensive?

What decisions are influenced by luck?

# 34

# What do people in your country disagree about?

What issues do people argue about?

What happens when people disagree?

What does friendly disagreement look like?

What is the worst kind of disagreement?

What political issues cause disagreement?

Do people fight about sports?

Are there generational disagreements?

Are there regional disagreements?

# 35

# How do people speak differently in different parts of your country?

How many languages are spoken in your country?

What are the main languages?

What are accents like?

Where do people speak the purest language?

Who has the most accent?

What stereotypes are associated with accents?

Do older people speak differently than younger?

Do rural people speak differently than city?

# 36

# What do college students do for fun?

What activities do college students do for fun?

Is fun a part of school or separate?

How much time do they have for fun?

Do they travel?

What games do they play?

When do they have fun?

Where do they go?

What is unique about college fun?

# 37

# What kind of music do teenagers listen to?

What is typical teenager music?

Is there a music industry for teenagers?

Are there famous teen musicians?

What variations of music do teens listen to?

What has changed about teen music in 20 years?

Do parents approve of teen music?

How important is music to a teenager?

Do teens listen to music from other countries?

# 38

# How are national leaders chosen?

What is the process of appointing national leaders?

How long has this been the process?

What are the advantages of this process?

What are the disadvantages?

What do you call the highest leader?

What makes a great leader?

What makes a poor leader?

When is a leader finished?

# 39

# How do you communicate with your head?

What are the meanings of facial expressions?

What can you communicate with your eyes?

What can you communicate with your nose?

What can you communicate with you mouth?

How can you communicate by moving your head?

What should you not do with your head or face?

What does eye contact mean?

When do you not make eye contact?

# 40

# What is rude when you are eating?

What is not ok while you are eating?

What noises are rude?

What is rude to say while you are eating?

When have you eaten too much?

What is rude at a formal meal that is usually ok?

How do you get food to your plate?

How do you show you are finished?

Who is the most important person at a meal?

# 41

# What are people afraid of?

What things do people fear?

Are people afraid to die?

Are some places scarier than others?

What makes a place scary?

Do people believe in ghosts, spirits etc.?

What makes a person scary?

What do you think is the most common fear?

Are fears different from previous generations?

# 42

# What has changed in the last 20 years?

Politics?

Economy?

Fashion?

Education?

Lifestyle?

Language?

Art/Music?

Other?

# 43

# Why do parents get upset with their children?

What behaviors upset parents?

What might a child say to upset his/her parent?

How are mothers and fathers different?

Do parents get upset about school performance?

How do parents respond when they are upset?

What is a good response?

What is a bad response?

How do children respond to upset parents?

# 44

# Why do children get upset with their parents?

What do parents do that upset their children?

How do children show they are upset?

How do teenagers show they are upset?

What do people think when they see a child cry?

How do parents respond to upset children?

What is bad behavior?

Is parenting different in public than private?

How has parenting changed over time?

# 45

# What do parents want for their kids?

What is most important about a child's future?

Good education?

Good money?

Happiness?

Family?

Position?

Mobility?

Something else?

# 46

# What is divorce like?

How do people get divorced?

How common is divorce?

What happens to children after divorce?

Is divorce expensive?

Is it common to re-marry?

Do people often marry several times?

What are considered reasons for divorce?

What are the social implications of divorce?

# 47

# What is crime like?

How bad is crime in your country?

What are the most common crimes?

What are the worst crimes?

Is there organized crime?

What areas have the most crime?

What areas have the least crime?

What are penalties for different crimes?

How has crime changed over the years?

# 48

# What is the impact of drugs?

Are drugs a major problem in your country?

Who takes drugs?

Who sells drugs?

What are the penalties for taking drugs?

What are the penalties for selling drugs?

How common are drugs?

When do people start using drugs?

How do people stop using drugs?

# 49

# What is a good gift to take to a home you are visiting?

Is it good to take a gift to a home you are visiting?

What is a good gift?

What is a bad gift?

Is it ok to take food?

What will people think if you don't take a gift?

How will people respond?

What is too expensive?

What is too cheap?

# 50

# How do poor people live?

Where do poor people live?

Who are the poorest people?

What problems come from poverty?

What is considered poor?

Who helps poor people?

What are the causes of poverty?

What do poor people do to survive?

How do people respond to the poor?

# 51

# How do rich people live?

Where do rich people live?

Who are the richest people?

What problems come from wealth?

What is considered rich?

How do people get rich?

How does wealth change people?

How to rich people help others?

How do people respond to the rich?

# 52

# What are the best places to visit in your country?

What are the most beautiful places?

What places have historical significance?

Where do tourists go?

What do tourists not know about?

How do people travel from place to place?

Where is the best food?

What places are not good?

What are the birthplaces of famous people?

# 53

# What makes you proud about your country?

What are your countries greatest accomplishments?

Who are famous people from your country?

What inventions have come from your country?

What is best about being from your country?

What is something that most people don't know?

How does your country help other countries?

What are people from your country good at?

What in your history makes you proud?

# 54

# How do you greet people?

How do you greet someone that you just met?

How do you greet someone that you know?

How do you greet a very good friend?

How do you greet a family member?

What words do you use to greet someone?

How is a casual greeting different from formal?

How do you show respect to an important person?

What is an inappropriate greeting?

# 55

# How does a person become famous?

What are some different ways to become famous?

How long does it take?

Who are the most famous people?

What is the best way to become famous?

What is the worst way to become famous?

Who is the most famous person you have met?

Do people want to become famous?

What has changed about being famous over time?

# 56

# What do people from your country wish was different?

What do people wish was different?

About the economy?

About the government?

About the geography?

About the climate?

About the culture?

About the food?

Other?

# 57

# How do families make decisions?

Is there a main decision maker in a family?

Who is that?

Do parents have conversation about decisions?

Do they talk to the kids?

Who has the final say?

How are families different in decision making?

What is the role of extended family?

How has decision making changed over time?

# 58

# How do people exercise?

What are the most common forms of exercise?

Do people exercise alone or with others?

How much money do people pay to stay healthy?

Why do people exercise?

Who exercises?

When do people exercise?

Where do people exercise?

How is exercise valued?

# 59

# How do you choose a name for your children?

Who chooses a name for children?

What is the process of choosing a name?

What makes a good name?

Do names have meaning?

Are names connected to family?

Do some names sound better than others?

Are some names for older people?

What are the most common names?

# 60

## How do people express happiness?

What expressions of happiness are common?

Smiling/laughing?

Jumping/dancing?

Loudness?

Crying?

Hugging?

Words of happiness?

Other?

# 61

# How do people express sadness?

What expressions of sadness are common?

Crying quietly (holding it in)?

Crying loudly?

Quietness?

When is it ok to express sadness?

When is it not ok to express sadness?

How do people respond to sadness?

How comfortable are people with sadness?

# 62

# How do people express disappointment?

What expressions of disappointment are common?

Body language?

Noises?

Words?

How do parents express disappointment?

Teachers?

Children?

Bosses?

# 63

# How do you put your children to bed?

What are bedtime routines?

Who puts the children to bed?

What time do children go to sleep?

What time do they wake up?

Do children take naps during the day?

What do you say to children when they go to bed?

Do you have bedtime songs?

Do you tell stories?

# 64

# What foods are only for breakfast?

Is breakfast hot or cold?

What are breakfast foods?

What are breakfast drinks?

What time do you eat breakfast?

Do you ever eat breakfast food for dinner?

Who prepares breakfast?

What is different if you eat breakfast out?

What has changed about breakfast over the years?

# 65

## What makes a good leader?

What makes a good government leader?

What makes a good company leader?

What makes a good community leader?

What makes a good athletic leader?

What makes a bad leader?

How important is character for a leader?

How important is age?

How important is experience?

# 66

## What time do you eat?

How many times a day do you eat?

What time is your first meal of the day?

What time is your last meal of the day?

Who eats with you?

What do you eat in the morning?

What do you eat at night?

What is too late to eat?

What is different about different meals?

# 67

# Who are the funniest people in your country?

Who do people think are funny?

What is funny about those people?

What people have the best sense of humor?

What people are laughed at the most?

Do you have comedians?

Are comedians respected?

How is humor used to influence people?

How important is humor?

# 68

# What is a song that almost everyone in your country knows?

Celebration song?

Traditional song?

A song that a mother sings to a child?

The national song or anthem?

What are the words?

What is the meaning?

When do you sing this song?

What is the history of the song?

# 69

## What is something that the people of your country wish was different?

Politics?

Economy?

Geography?

Climate?

Why do they wish it was different?

How could it be different?

Are people hopeful that it will change?

How long would it take to change?

# 70

## Who is your family?

What does the word "family" mean?

Who is included in family?

Only relatives or close friends?

Who is not family?

How are decisions made in a family?

When does a family begin?

What changes when people are married?

Who lives in a home together?

# 71

# What makes a mother proud?

School?

Sport?

Good behavior?

Music?

How does a mother show she is proud?

What does a mother say when she is proud?

How do mothers talk to each other when proud?

How are mothers different from each other?

# 72

# What pressure do teenagers have?

Pressure to do well in school?

Pressure to impress friends?

Pressure to be good?

Pressure to be bad?

Where does the most pressure come from?

What is it like?

When does the hardest pressure begin?

When does the pressure end?

# 73

# How do you express appreciation?

How do you thank someone?

What words are used?

What gestures, body language etc. are used?

Is repayment necessary?

Are gifts given to show appreciation

What words or actions are not ok?

What happens if appreciation is not shown?

What happens if there is too much appreciation?

# 74

# How do you express anger?

To a family member?

To a friend?

To a co-worker?

To a boss?

To a stranger?

When do people yell?

When does it get physical?

What is not ok?

# 75

## Why do you work?

To make more money?

To have nice things?

For your family?

To be happy?

For status?

Because you love your job?

Because you have no choice?

How has this changed over time?

# 76

# What traditions are a part of becoming an adult?

When does a person become an adult?

Are there any celebrations for entering adulthood?

What food/drink is involved?

What advice is given?

What freedoms come with adulthood?

What responsibilities come with adulthood?

How does a young person show they are ready?

Not ready?

# 77

# What ages are important?

What are "special" ages?

Why are they special?

How are they acknowledged?

What changes at those ages?

Are there special celebrations?

What are the most important ages from 1 to 10?

What are the most important ages from 10 to 20?

What are the most important ages for adults?

# 78

# What is a scary story that most people would know?

A legendary story of a ghost or spirit?

A true story from history?

A story used to get children to obey?

A fairy tale?

Who tells scary stories?

Who are they told to?

What is the purpose?

Do people believe them?

# 79

## How are children disciplined?

What methods of discipline are used?

What methods of discipline are not used?

Who disciplines a child?

Can people outside of family discipline children?

How do families differ?

What is the purpose of discipline?

When do children stop being disciplined?

Has discipline changed over time?

# 80

## Dancing:  Who? When? Where? Why? How?

What role does dancing play in your culture?

What are some different forms of dance?

Who dances?

What occasions would people dance?

How do dances vary by region?

How do dances vary by groups of people?

How do dances vary by generation?

Are there disagreements about dancing?

# 81

# What is different about an important meal and a regular meal?

Who makes a meal important?

Where is an important meal served?

How are important people distinguished?

What is different about the food?

Do people wear different clothing?

Are the drinks different?

How are people seated?

When is an important meal over?

# 82

# How do you shop for food?

What kind of markets do you shop at for food?

What different kinds of markets are available?

Who shops at which kind of market?

What foods are expensive?

What foods are cheap?

Can food be delivered to your home?

How much time do you spend shopping for food?

How has buying food changed over time?

# 83

# How do you start a fight?

What often causes people to fight?

Are there certain topics that cause people to fight?

How do people usually fight? Yelling? Punching?

What groups of people often fight?

What age groups are most likely to fight?

What do nearby people do if they see a fight?

What happens if a man hits a woman?

What happens if a woman hits a man?

# 84

# How do you insult someone?

What is a common insult?

What are people compared to as an insult?

How does someone respond if they are insulted?

What people are often insulted?

What people should never be insulted?

Is it different between age groups?

What is the most offensive insult?

Can insults be a sign of affection between friends?

# 85

# How does your country feel about my country?

What do people in your country think about mine?

What stereotypes do they have?

What do they think is strange or weird?

What do they appreciate?

What do old people think about my country?

Young people?

Where do people get their ideas?

How have these ideas changed over time?

# 86

# How do you bargain?

Is it ok to bargain (argue about the price)?

What products are ok to bargain for?

What products are not ok to bargain?

How do you know if you are getting a good deal?

Who is good at bargaining?

What are the rules of bargaining?

What happens when foreigners bargain?

How has bargaining changed over time?

# 87

## What treats do children get excited about?

What candies or sweets do children love?

What does it taste like?

Where do you get it?

Is it homemade or bought?

Where do children want to go for fun?

What happens there?

Is it expensive or cheap?

How have these things changed over time?

# 88

# How do you find out what is happening?

How do you learn about what is happening?

In the world?

In your nation?

In your hometown/city/village?

What outlets are used (TV, internet, paper etc.)?

Where do people talk about news?

What do they say?

How has this changed over time?

# 89

# What makes your country great?

What are the best things about your country?

Are people patriotic?

How do people express patriotism?

What are the symbols of patriotism?

How is your country celebrated?

What historical events are celebrated?

What foods do you eat to celebrate your country?

How has this changed over time?

# 90

## What is a famous poem or tongue twister?

What is a poem that everyone would know?

A tongue twister?

Where do they come from?

When do you learn them?

What variations are there?

How fast can you say the tongue twister?

What are the forms of poetry?

Who are the most famous poets and writers?

# 91

# What is legendary?

What historical stories are most famous?

How are they exaggerated?

Are they debated or controversial?

Why did they become famous stories?

What variations are there?

How are the stories retold?

How are they remembered or respected?

How has this changed over time?

# 92

# Who are the most famous criminals in your country?

What crimes did they commit?

When did it happen?

Did they get caught?

What was the penalty for their crime?

Why are they so famous?

How do people feel about them now?

What was the impact of their crime?

What changed because of them?

# 93

# What is the meaning of your country's flag?

What are the parts of your flag?

What are the different colors?

What are the different symbols?

What do the colors represent?

What do the symbols represent?

What is the history of your flag?

How do people feel when they see the flag?

Where do people raise the flag?

# 94

# Who takes care of people who cannot care for themselves?

Who takes care of mentally disabled people?

Physically disabled?

What does the government do to help?

What do families and friends do?

Are there businesses that help?

How do most people respond to disabled people?

What are the challenges?

How has this changed over time?

# 95

# What is marriage?

What is the process that leads to marriage?

What role do the parents play?

What is the relationship before marriage?

How do you ask someone to marry you?

What are the laws about marriage?

How long is an engagement?

How is a marriage ended?

How has this changed over time?

# 96

# How do you address people?

What names or titles are used to address people?

How do you address men and women differently?

Are there special titles for older people?

For important people?

Who gets a title of importance?

Who does not get a title?

How important is a title?

How has this changed over time?

# 97

# Who are your most famous celebrities?

Who are the most famous people in your country?

Actors?

Singers?

Other celebrities?

How did they get famous?

What are their personalities?

What do people think of them?

What are the different opinions about them?

# 98

# How do people feel about animals?

How important are pets?

What animals are pets?

Do you have zoos?

What are they like?

What animals are eaten?

What animals are not eaten?

Does this vary from place to place?

Has this changed over time?

# 99

# How much time off do you get?

How much time do average people get off of work?

What do they do with that time?

Do they get paid for that time?

Do they often travel?

When do people travel?

Who travels together?

Is it common for people to travel internationally?

Has this changed over time?

# Note

When you have asked ALL 99 Questions to
ALL of your global friends . . . start over.
See what you learn the second time.

Never stop asking.


Thanks for using this resource.

# Jerry Jones

Jerry lives on the East side of China with his wife and two children. His job and his life's passion are to equip global people. You can learn more about him and get access to other great resources for expats, repats and more at:

**www.thecultureblend.com**

Made in the USA
Coppell, TX
19 February 2020

15983676R00066